This pro
In the ea
I moved

Well-meaning idiots
They taught me as they had been taught
Some of which turned out to be very useful

Then for some reason
I could never understand
They turned me over to a state run
Indoctrination Center
It was a 12-year sentence
But I got two years off for
bad behavior

The last time I was in the dean of boys office
Was the first time we agreed on anything
He told my mother that as far as he was concerned
My education was complete

I spent a lot of time down at
Rubys candy store
Drinking cherry cokes and
Smoking loosies (3 for 5¢)
My big life plan was to join the Navy
As soon as I was 18
Some plan that turned out to be
The Navy was a bigger pain in the ass
Than the Indoctrination Center
My vision for travel and adventure
Turned out to be
Three duty stations in Maryland and
Drunken weekends in DC
Things improved after
I got out of boot camp
I like working on airplanes
And I could get wasted
At the enlisted men's club
Almost every night
My $76 per mo lasted nicely
Draft beers were only 10 cents
And I could buy a carton of
Lucky Strikes for a dollar
But then I got interested in Playing poker
And I wound up being broke
Most of the time
My mother would only send me
Five dollars at a time
And I had to do a lot of whining
To even get that

Fast Forward to 1961

I was working for my
mother and father
At their steel rule die shop
in Brooklyn N Y
Our gross sales that year
Were less than $20,000
Then with absolutely no idea
Of what I was doing
I got married and we had
Two kids in the first 3 years
We were very lucky to live
Near my wife's family
We were almost completely
Ignorant and inexperienced
Their help and support
Was a lifesaver

Then came 1969
I had worked as a salesman for
CUTCO cutlery and
Hearthstone Ins. Co.
Selling $3.00 accident policies
Both careers ended badly
And I was back at the
Mom and pop die shop

A Moment of Insight

I was so sick with bronchitis
That I had to sleep sitting up
During the night
I awoke and took
A few tokes on my
Iso medihaler
To relieve my asthma
Then I fired up a Winston
As I sat there coughing
And thinking
I had this great
Breakthrough awareness
This shit don't work if
I keep it up I will be
Forced to Leave the planet

And so started my 45 year quest
For knowledge understanding
And a better way

Live to the limit
Of your knowledge
Expand your knowledge
To the limit
Of your life
Ayn Rand

1970

I stopped drinking alcohol and smoking
(for a while) and started jiggling
My 210 pounds
Up and down Cartaret Avenue
I subscribed to Prevention Magazine,
Read books by Robert Rodell
And listened to Carlton Fredericks
On the radio
As I reduced the disgusting
Nonfood substances I
Ingested
The jiggling turned into jogging
My head seemed to
Settle down a little
The depression wasn't As deep or as long
As it has been in the past
And the anger was not as
Out-of-control
From the high ground of my
75th year I can see
What a large roll Lady Luck plays
In how things come out
Just when I needed study time most
The Arab oil embargo came along
It got my fat ass out of the car
And into a Public Service
Bus and subway
For my daily commute
From Cartaret, NJ to Brooklyn

I had subscribed to the Classic Book Club
The first to arrive was

Meditations by Marcus Aurelius

Because a thing is difficult
For you
Do not therefore suppose
It is beyond
Your power on the contrary
If anything is possible and proper
For a man to do
Assume that it must fall within
Your own capacity

I have carried it with me
All over the world
It gave me a whole new perspective
It's not them or that
It's me
It's not what's going on
But how I choose to interpret
What's going on
That determines the kind of
Reaction I create
I didn't have the skills
To do that but
The knowledge offered hope for
A way out
Of all the misery
And mind storms
That sucked up
My energy and time

Lady fortune smiled on me
The day I opened that book
If you haven't read it
Stop everything
And get a copy today
I read half a page most mornings

It's not what I know
It's what I can remember I know
When I need to know it

I always know I should
Chew my food
And not spit it all over others
It's just when I'm eating
I forget it
I will
Remember what I know
When I need to know it
Stand straight-Breath-
pay attention-stop rushing
Don't interrupt people-refuckinglax-
Smile Ask questions-
Don't talk so much-Stop boasting
Brush your teeth
This head fixing work
Is a long drawn out
Project

1976

I grew up in Brooklyn and
Woodhaven Queens NYC
Of all the good Fortune
I have been blessed with
Spending the summers on
My grandfathers farm
Was the most formative
I learned to churn butter-
Fix fences drive a team of
Horses-milk cows-
Shoot a gun pick currents-
Beans and blueberry's
Kill and clean a chicken
Or a bass build a tree house
And damn up the crick
Pickle cucumbers
And shovel cow and horse shit
And following coon dogs
As they howled there
Way through the night

Unloading hay

What a trip
65 years ago
And I still get goose bumps
Thinking about it
The team wasn't nuts about
Walking backwards
So to back them up the ramp
Into the barn with a full load
Took patience and skill

Grandfather would lower
A large fork that was
Attached to a trolley on the ceiling
Then while he unhooked
The horses from the wagon
I would jump on the fork
Till it was completely
Buried in the load
Then I would set the barbs
And he would hook the horses up
As soon as the hay

Reached the trolley
It would move on a rail
To the other end of the barn
Then I would get to
Pull the rope
That released the barbs
Down it came
With a big whoosh
HOW EXCITING
Then we would climb up and
Level it off and do it again
It usually took 4 lifts
To empty the wagon

Back to 1976
Mom and Pop had retired
And I was making
A very modest living
Making steel rule dies
And die cutting things
For other company's
From across the universe
Destiny whispered
Now
My country uncle called and said
The old Bordon's Creamery
Near my grandfather' farm is
FOR SALE

And they only want
$1,000.00
My heart jumped around in my chest
There is no way to describe how badly
I wanted to get out of that
God-forsaken city
But we didn't have a $1,000.00
Rose my wife's sister who was always

Loving and generous with us
Offered to lend us the money
So I bought a old 22 foot GMC truck
And the adventure of my life
Went into high gear

I never drove a truck before
So I found an empty
Parking lot and practiced
Backing up
When I thought I knew
What I was doing I drove
To the shop and after 4 or 5 tries
I got backed into the alley
For loading
Now in my excited ignorance
I loaded it right to the roof
With no consideration
For how heavy it was getting
As I crept out of the alley

The cab started to fill up
With smoke
It smoked a little
When it was empty but
But with a full load it was like a
Mosquito sprayer
What incredible good luck that I
Could go 250 miles and not
Get stopped by the police
I added oil 3 times and sat
For 30 min to cool off
After the long climb over
Lexington notch
Finely I backed into the new
Loading my cousin George had
Built on to the old creamery

I can still feel the joy and relief
As I lit up a Winston
And cracked open a can of beer
I forgot to remember that
I didn't do that shit any more
But this was a very special occasion

I sit here trying to find words
To express the way I felt
That evening as I walked around the
Quiet old Creamery

AND DREAMED OF
THE FUTURE
I would create here
Only a few times in my life
Have I experienced such
Joy and gratitude

Now for the rest of my life
I will live here
Where my mothers family
Settled 210 years ago
Every day as I drive
By the old farm
I reflect on my great good fortune
Three more truck loads to go
One of my new neighbors did
A complete engine job
Quickly and inexpensively
I was back on the road again
In just a few days
A rigger I knew sympathized
With my escape
Gave me a brother in law price
To move my 3 die cutting presses
Out of the War zone
And then the last load and all my
Crap was out of Brooklyn
FOREVER
No more bus and subway study times
So I took time almost every day
To study-exercise and write
No meditation for another 5 years

1983
Greenleaf Steel Rule Die Corp

**Had become the largest manufacture of
Dollhouse kits in the world
With 45 employees and $4.2 million in sales**

I have to give a lot credit to my first 2 wives

**And Napoleon Hill
Without their effort and his book
Think and Grow Rich
This would never have happened
Once again Lady Fortune
smiled on my busyness
The intelligent motivated people that
Joined me in this endeavor
Managed all the day to day operations**

This left me free to do trade shows
Travel
Study-exercise-meditate and write

The following are some journal
Entries from that period

New York City
5-13-95

A trunk of puppets is the way
Robert deRopp described
This affliction that we all share
Mechanical puppets
Brought to center stage by
Forces unknown
And probably unknowable
Then quickly replaced
By another with a
Completely different case
To make and "we" "I " pace
Around backstage
Wondering what's going on
And what's going to
Happen next
This whole performance can be
At least partially
Brought under control
It only takes 20 or 30 years
Of training
Never give up

Newark, NJ
5-20-95

Manic-depressive bipolar schizophrenic
Obsessive-compulsive
And many other terms that describe
States of chemically base awareness
This whole situation cannot even be
Comprehended without understanding an
Enormously complicated series of
Chemical inter reactions
Many tiny changes can totally
Disrupt the whole process
Some simple examples are
The introduction of a
Very small quantity of strychnine or LSD
Or the absence of vitamin B12 vitamin D
And fitness-hydration-sleep-temperature
All play their role in balance
Chemically based biological balance
Is absolutely essential before anyone can
Consistently experience a reliable
State of being
These are not the only requisites
But beyond a doubt they must be the first
I will continue to study and exercise
And bring about a very high state
Of fitness and balanced health
Then maybe I can make some
Real progress in evolving myself
A computer will only work correctly on
110 V 60 cycle alternating current
Nothing else will work

Margaretville, NY
5-21-95

Consider
How little time in your life
Has been spent in a state of
Optimum health
Has there been any
It takes a tough man
To make it tender chicken
That's what Frank Purdue
The torturer of billions said
And if you want to really want
To make progress
You have to give yourself
Every edge
Pull out all the stops
Live fully all paths and
Every activity has
The same potential
If utilized appropriately

Nashville, TN
6-12-95

This energy that propels me is
An unbroken chain
Since the primordial soup started
Squirming around
Not one microsecond gap in the
Billions of years of change
This power has continually
Moved through
Higher and higher levels of Organization

And this morning it pulses loudly
In my being
I feel fit-strong and eager to organize
And evolves myself a little more today
I have played my role in history
The life force has been pasted forward
In time
And my daughter in turn
Has done the same
All living things play their part
And are propelled by the same
Unseen force
Most humans do not nurture this power
And many do things to subvert it
By age 60 they are dull shadows
Of what was possible
What a well-kept secret
How great the possibilities
And how little most of us make of them
The oak tree always acts
In it's own best interest
And grows steadily
In stature and strength
As the generations

Of humans pass
But we hire
Organizations of activity
Spend as much time
Breaking things down
As we do growing and nurturing
This short-term possibility
How extraordinary I can maintain this Primordial fire
On an incredibly wide range of raw materials
There are much more for filling levels of Organization
For me but it will require a very usual level of
Balance and effort
Little things make a big difference
If I am to actualize even a small part
It will take knowledge discipline and effort

The stage is set
For billions of years this life force
Has been moving toward me
And today I have the possibility of
Bringing it to a little higher level of Organization
Big deal you still have a 10 pound roll of fat
Around your waist and a lot more in your head
All is well

Schenevus, NY
6-14-95

Health and wisdom are
An output of
All kinds of inputs
The decades fly by
And things accumulate
My great plans
Reveal their flaws
While I enjoy
The many benefits of my
Lucky brakes

Margaretville, NY
6-29-95

The power of managing each instant
Cannot be overstated
How quickly things accumulate
When I focus all my efforts
On a single outcome
Like present moment awareness
Everything becomes a rung in the ladder
I bull shit myself about climbing
Driving-walking-waiting-eating
No better no worse
Only this
Just now

Margaretville, NY
7-9-95

I just read something I wrote in 1992
Same crap different year
But today is going to be different
I will breathe deeply and stay peaceful
How simple
That's all there is to it
I have wasted so much life force
Well everything in its season
I guess I wasn't ready till today
That's a lot better than never
Thank God

I've been getting really sick of
Beating the shit out of my self
Yesterday was enough already
Pain-tension-helplessness-
Catastrophic expatiation
Glad to have all that behind me

Schenevus, NY
7-31-14

I hope you are finding this noise
Interesting and maybe motivating
My purpose is to demonstrate
How large, long term and rewarding
This fixing my head project
Has been and is

Marcus Aurelius
Sometime in the 0160s

Take it that you died today
And your life's story is ended
Hence forward regard what future time
May be given you as surplus
And live it out in harmony
With nature

Margaretville, NY
1-1-96

And then there was another year
I will rededicate myself to my
Most important project
The creation of a second to second
State of awareness and gratitude
For my little drop of time
In the ocean of eternity
All is well
That's all
Study, meditate, breathe, do yoga
And stay aware of how good I have it
Every second life begins anew
I cannot function outside of this
Great blanket of ignorance
That covers me but still
Within those confines
Much more is possible
Because I finally have learned that the
Thoughts I permit myself to have
Create my experience and
Shape my destiny
I am a creative force
I will peacefully reshape myself
And my world
That was
Another new year's resolve

1996

My son and daughter took over the business
And I packed up some camping gear
In my 1991 pickup truck and headed west
After several weeks of "camping"
(mostly in cheap motels)
I pulled into Johnny Walker Trailer Sales
In Lost Wages, NV & bought a well-used
18' Prowler fifth wheel trailer
They insisted I spend the first night there
Good idea, I had lots of questions
Then off I went with my new home

Chester, CA
5-15-96

Effort   Effort
Make the effort
Forget the past stop hanging on
To all the people, places and things
Cut the anchor rope if you are
Hauling it in
Then you'll just have to carry it
Around with you
Use all your available energy
For the work at hand
Which is always and only now
Freedom – enlightenment
Presents

Hyatt Lake, OR
5-19-96

Deepak Chopra says
Stop alcohol and caffeine
Eat the largest meal at mid day
So on I go expecting what I want
And getting what I deserve
The outcome perfectly befits the input
No matter how I feel about it
Well it's 5 o'clock in Schenevus he says
As he uncorked a bottle of Rosemont Shiraz
I'll take a short break from all this heavy thinking

Mendocino, CA
6-3-96

Use time to sow the seeds of
Future harvests
Start now
This will be the
Smoothest posture flow of all time
Slowly - precisely –
With more attention than ever before
And then on to my future life's work
Filling blank books with bullshit
Dean the wordsmith
If nothing else
They will make a great bonfire
At my hundredth birthday party

Fallbrock, CA
6-15-96

This time alone has enabled me to see
The enormity of my dysfunction
Or maybe that's how
Dysfunctional everybody is
But that is not my problem
My problem keeps growing hair
Or at least for a while
What new steps can I take
What can I do to
Summon up the required effort
Read more eat less who the fuck knows
Ease up - Breath deep - relax
Life is better than it's ever been
I'll see if there is any wine left in the closet

060s
Marcus Aurelius

You cannot hope to be a scholar
But what you can do is curb arrogance
What you can do is
Rise above pleasure and pains
You can be superior
To the lore of popularity
You can keep your temper
With the foolish and ungrateful
And yes even care for them

Bishop, CA
6-16-96

So all is well
It's 6 AM and I'm way behind schedule already
I got caught up in all these books
That I keep reading over and over
I have to write down these
Great insights that I just had
Meditate, practice yoga
With much concentration and awareness
Exercise, eat breakfast
Then bike into town for some supplies
Then I should introduce myself to the
Lady with the van
That pulled in last night in the
Campsite across from me
She had a very alluring bumper sticker
Vegetarians taste better
I am curious as to whether
There is any truth to that
You never know when the next
Adventure will start
Back to recording insights
Effort – I'm just not putting in enough effort
I've created this comfortable
Little environment on wheels
With a great daily agenda
Study, write, practice yoga, meditate, bicycle
Like a hamster in an exercise wheel
The missing ingredient is real effort
The mission is large and the time is short

Cattle Camp, CA
6-19–96

The good news is
There's always another chance
Till that one day without a sunset
The slate is clean
My mind is keen
The light is green
So I will reeve up the machine
And most likely drop the ball again
But there is some new ingredients
In the soup
Time alone - a solid schedule of
Daily training
Few distractions and
Focusing on this project more fully
All I "have" to do is breathe and die
Just about everything else is a choice of
How   Where   When   What
So choose to be grateful and present
In all activities

Cattle Camp, CA
6-20-96

All there is, is awareness
And time framed things to be aware of
This is my central mission
To peacefully escalate my effort
And just be aware
Change will come
This trailer and selling the business
Are cornerstones in what is now possible for me
I can learn to live skillfully
Eliminate involvements and practice awareness
And move slowly into my life's work
Writing and teaching
But only when I have become the master of myself

Klamath River CA
6-21-96

Wisdom seems to be easing its way
Under my trailer door
I biked into the town of Weed yesterday
Played no limit lowball all afternoon
Then I had a great dinner and
Two glasses of wine
At the natural café
The full moon lit my ride home
And illuminated
Mount Shasta in the distance
That was all very nice
But what does it have to do with
My purpose
So now I will make the bed

A Pinewoods North of Reno, NV
6-25-96

Effort, supreme effort is the ticket to mastery
I study, meditate and do yoga
Day after day and make no progress
Become one pointed like the rays of the sun
When focused throughout magnifying glass
The present is the magnifying glass
My power and everything I have learned
Is the sun
And I sit in the shade drinking wine
How incredibly large these
Dormant possibilities are
That I muddle around in
That's all no rush-no tension-no dawdling
Smart-crisp-well directed movement
This is making the bed
The most important next step
In my path of evolving myself
I'll carry on till I'm carried out

Reno, NV
6-26-96

Consider this
The earths took shape
About 4 billion years ago
And I will certainly be
Dead in less than 70 years
The flickering light of my perception is a
Short-term minor event,
But it's all I've got
The only project
That makes any sense to me
Is to evolve myself into a being of choice
To learn and practice creating
A wholesome state of mind in any setting

Trail, British Columbia
7-9-96

No practice for the last two days
Things are not going in the right direction
Last night I spilled coffee grounds in the sink
And this morning I lost my pen
Some practice of awareness
Is this just some kind of vacation
Am I just driving around for the hell of it
Like watching TV or shooting pool
Get with the program
This may be your last chance
So be here now and
Fearlessly
Peacefully
Persistently
Totally

Breathe-exercise-and do yoga
Then go jump in the cold Columbia River
More later if I don't drown

Back in NY for a short visit

Schenevus, NY
8-17-96

The door of liberation is a jar
The bright light of salvation
Is just perceptible around the edge
And I muddle around in stories of
Shoulda-coulda-woulda
Sail boat-new house looking cool
And the big possibility's slip into the
Nothingness that is the past
There is no past except in my head
In the best case that's a
Short-term problem
So now with great attention
I will study- practice yoga and meditate

Schenevus, NY
8-20-95

Don't believe any of this bull shit
I have been staining these pages with
I haven't listened to the silence
For more than 3 minutes in a row
In my whole life
And maybe I've eaten 2 muffins
And noticed the whole process
But hope rains eternal
There's still a chance
Effort
I will exert enormous effort
No excuses   No delays
Now

Schenevus, NY
8-27-96

Sloppen the same slops
If nothing else my appreciation is
Greater than ever
And so is my understanding of how
Temporary all this bull shit is
Leaves in the fall wind
The lawful out flow of all the inflows
10,000 years ago the ice was a mile deep
Right here where i sit
Or was that a 100,000 years
Split vision
Watch Dean watching the activity
Watch the watcher
OR
Eat shit and die
OR
Eat health food and die
Or just fucking die and get it over with
Have a nice day

Schenevus, NY
8-29-96

My life is like
Eating an artichoke
The flavor and texture improve
As you approach the last morsel
It all seems like a dream this morning
A foggy memory of something that
Seemed real at the time
Lightning in the night sky
June fireflies
A late fall walk in the leaves
Dreams on my death bed
My perceptions of this Earth drama
Are turning inside out
Upside down
Leave it all behind in the misty past
That will soon be no past
I'm a stranger in a familiar place
All is well

Schenevus, NY
10-5-96

The last train is leaving the station
And I'm standing on the platform
With both thumbs up my ass
Looking the other way
Extraordinary good fortune got me here
I have just an instant to get on board
One "Star Trek"Adventure
Commander Pecard was considering a
Earth bound job in oceanographer's
I had this strong vision that if I had
The opportunity to command a star ship
I would say good by to everyone I know
And leave forever
Without hesitation
I will leave forever
Maybe this sunny September day
If not soon
I have been placed squarely before this
Opportunity of exploring the universe
The Star Ship is in orbit
The helm is mine for the taking
I can because I do
I do because I can
It's a crooked painful road
That got me to this juncture
The warm breeze whispers
Of Great Works
And this morning it roars in my ears
I will accept this mission
And press on
No matter what the price
The possibility of Transformation
Is within sight
The breeze reeks of it
The trees and the grass are vibrating
The stage is set

Schenevus NY
10-7-96

So about 30 minutes after
All that happy Bull shit
I got to my office stuck my head up my ass
And ran in circles all day
I'll start over
In this predawn silence I will
Study, practice yoga and meditate
And plan my escape from the
Deadly duo details and deadlines
Or is it myself I'm trying to escape from

Schenevus, NY
9-10-96

Today is the day
Of a whole new way
No shit I say
Today?
The sun is coming up
And I think I'm going to get
Another chance
One more day
Spent the same old way
Or maybe an epiphany
A new leaf
?

Schenevus, NY
9-14-96

Tick   Tick   Tick   Tick
The kitchen clock plays
Its fatal tune
Fall flies buzzing and dying
Like pepper on mashed potatoes
They speckle my white carpet
Wind chimes bright sun
Fat-thin-fit-weak
Dead forever soon
I think the flowers would look better
On the table by the window
Said the captain of Titanic
As the cold Atlantic came over the rail
All is well
And I always find something to think about
A fool in a hopeless fool's game
Trying to direct a cast of conflicting entities
That pull me in meany directions
But
I will persevere and prevail

Schenevus, NY
8-19-14

With all my bullshit theories these 2
Stand way above all the others
1 study-exercise-meditate
And Journal every day

2 Every instance there's always
Something I can do to improve things

The main thrust of my studies has
Always fallen under the
General heading of
Learning how to take care of myself

Make enough money Training my mind
Care and feeding
The priorities are always shifting as I
Learn and implement my latest theory
In the beginning
I was almost totally focused
On making enough money
Looking back that was probably
The right choice
I was very unhealthy and
Totally reactive but
Making enough money afforded me
The leisure time and resources
To study-learn to practice yoga-and
Exercise a lot
The focus was always shifting around
When business was good
I hardly thought about it
But when ever I got it screwed up
Because of some stupid decision I made
Most of my time would be spent studying
Working and thinking about fixing it

Not having *enough* money is a
Really big pain in the ass
But running around with
A head full of demons isn't much better
So I almost always made time for
Exercise and inspirational reading
Here at the midpoint of my eighth decade
I would like to find a few people
That would be interested in learning
Some helpful hints about how to live
And make the most of this great possibility
Life on earth
Now
Learning new things is great
I hope to keep it up for another 40 years
But remembering what I already know
When I need to use it
That's where change and new habits
Get real traction

Bolxom, VA
10-19-96

On the road at 3:45 this morning
I landed here at 11:30
Had a healthy lunch
A couple of glasses of wine
And slept with the Angels till 4:30pm
All is well
See every activity for what it is
A retraining opportunity
That's all
Let it take as long as it takes
But don't mope
There's only so much time left
Proceed only at ease
If tension or frenzy arise
Let up on the speed control
Or stop if necessary
I will often check my
Head state and posture
They are inextricably linked
Choreograph each activity
With smooth graceful movements
This is not securing the equipment
For transport
It's the high and holy work of
Self evolution
The possibilities lay in the quality
And attention given to the activity
Not the outcome

Benson, AZ
11-3-96

So I went on a travel spree and covered
1400 miles in two days
No study no exercise no meditation
No balance
Rush rush rush for what
To where
Why
Old demons die hard
And given just a little opening
They take over
Today is a new start
A perfect setting
NOW
I will stay here for a while
Study-do-yoga-write and meditate
57 years ago I dropped into time
Now is the time to learn how to live here
With a grateful heart and a peaceful mind
I will make the extra effort and stay at ease

Geezer City Trailer Park, Tucson AZ
11-11-96

I biked 50 miles Sat & Sun
Lost a few pounds
Won a holdem tournament
Depressed confused
What the hell am I doing
Living in a broken down old trailer
Surrounded with "seniors"
Oh I remember
I'm supposed to be working on my head
Not playing poker all day at the casino
A fresh start
Study Ouspensky Krishnamurti Gurdjieff
Practice yoga-meditate
Write about all the progress your making
The clock is ticking away the possibility's
And if I really work at it
I may make some meaningful chance
Either way All is Well

Agua Caliente, CA
1-1-97

More resolutions
John Fuchs said in the Book
Forty years after Grudiieff
Become a man of the world
Develop essence-strength-fortitude-
Personality-tact
Will-objectivity-total balance-
Adaptability-polish
Understanding of life's relationships
Able to play the correct role in every
Life situations
And I would add love-gratitude
Compassion-health and fitness
So what's the chances
You can't even remember to chew your food
NONE
If I continue these half-ass efforts
SMALL
If I give it my all
An oath
I will NEVER AGAIN
Allow negativity or depression
Now go make some coffee without spilling it

Agua Caliente Ca
1-5-97

Third day of a fast
Its clearer this morning than ever before
What an enormous undertaking this is
No one plays the piano in Carnegie Hall
Without many years of study and practice
And the dynamic components
Are a small fraction
Of what's involved in this project of
Self Mastery
Thousands of false starts
Doing the same stupid shit over and over
No hope but one
Observation
I have to see it before I can change it
Most of the time it's like trying to tell
What an elephant is by sticking my nose
Up its ass all I can say is it stinks
So I'll stand back as far as I can
And watch this process unfold
Then act decisively
The last time I stopped smoking
It was fairly easy
When I saw how destructive it is
And the same it will be with the rest of
My disharmonious ways
Observation   Awareness   Succession
Never relent

Just see it like learning to play a piano
Trial and success practice-practice
Everything is raw material for this undertaking
I will always remember my purpose
I'm not decorating the trailer door
I am creating my being
A single brick in the tower of
Self Mastery
The lower ones are set and secure
But the most current ones are vulnerable
They need time for the mortar to set
I will proceed with balance and awareness
And practice

Yuma, AZ
1-12-97

I awoke in a very powerful state
I have been studying for the last 2 1/2 hr
With a very high level of comprehension
Different days   Different energy's
All is well
It is very clear to me this morning
How vast and abundant are the
Possibilities
And how little I have made of it
Even if I can't see a mature corn stalk
In my minds eye
I know that if I plant-water-fertilize
And wait
This inevitable process will unfold
Abraham Lincoln said
I will prepare myself
And my work will appear
So on with the preparation
Yoga-mediation-exercise

Pahrump, NV
1-16-97

It doesn't matter much where I am
Its witch direction I heading that will
Determine my destiny
Don't give back an inch
Stand your ground
This coming week will show me if my
"Progress" is real or just more
Self delusion
I haven't missed a
Hobby Industry of America trade show
Since 1979 and it starts tomorrow
Family old friends and a long track record of
Eating and drinking too much

1-17-97

And once again my little "home"
Sits on the sacred ground of
Circus-Circus Casino and RV park
In high and holey freak show of
Lost Wages, NV
I have only one purpose
In this coming storm of
Activity and involvements
To use its energy to raise my game
To a whole new level
Tension free   I'll climb this tree
See how all this bull shit stands up

3AM the First Day of the show

I will be at ease and pay attention
That's all
Let everyone tend to there own business
And I'll tend to mine
Smile have fun
Maybe sell a few doll houses
Stay present and relaxed

4:30 the Second Day

So I ran my mouth in many
Grand pontifications on my extensive knowledge
Of everything
Maybe that's what happens
When you don't talk to any body for a while
A scene from Millmen's book Peaceful Warrior
Comes to mind
He was teaching a woman's gymnastic class
And they all must have all been on the rag
So he prayed to Jesus and Buddha for advice
And a voice replied that they would not have
Got themselves into such a situation
High and holey wisdom
Get the fuck out town wile your still alive

Third morning

So I went back for another dose
How difficult it is to see my disharmonious ways
Lost in a fog of theories and opinions
They are road blocks in my path
Judging and evaluating
Everyone everything
He's fat she's stupid that's so crazy
If only-you never-I always-
Why do you do that shit

Today
I will use
"I have no opinion on this"
When ever I here any of that bull shit
Echoing around in my head I'll remember
"I have no opinion on this"
It's none of my business
My business is to uncover and construct
The wisdom and skill that will enable me
To be of service to my fellow beings

03:30 Last morning in L V

I don't know what to do
Should I go to China and see the
Three gorges before they fill with water
Walk the toe paths
Carved into the canyon walls
Fly "home" practice yoga
The night wind shakes
My cozy little trailer
I'm snug and warm and as at home
As I've ever been anywhere
All my dreams and schemes seem
Silly and child like
Die cutting-dollhouses-book writing
The center of creative possibility's
I just lay here looking at the blank page
My thoughts flashing all over
In search of some kind of understanding
Change
Everything is changing all the time
In just 135 years
Every single living human
Will be dead for ever
Go back to sleep

Schenevus, NY
8-14-14

Now please consider the following
Deeply
1 Daily practice
Study- exercise -meditation and writing
2 Present moment awareness
To be grateful and remember that I can
Do something each instance to improve things
Come away from this stupid book
With these two concepts
And you can transform your life

7-29-14
The Last Stand

(home?)
And in just the flash of an eye it was 2007
My grandfather left me 40 acres
And in 1991 I built a house here
For me and my mother and father
It was the first time
They owned their own home
But only for a short time
They both died within a year
I married an old acquaintance
At the end of 1997
Over time we built
Chicken coop-goat shed
And a workshop/garage
She spent her time
Growing vegetables-flowers
Milking goat
And making cheese and yogurt
I took care of the
Chickens and did most of the
Harvesting and freezing of vegetables
Also studying-meditating-writing
And exercising
And playing way way too much
Internet poker
Next I'll play you some of the very
Insightful bullshit
That I wrote between tournaments at
Party Poker and Poker Stars
So you can see my great leaps in
Wisdom-knowledge and consciousness

The Last Stand 2014

I read through four months worth of
The same crap over and over again
Try harder-start again-pay attention
Brush your teeth-chew your food-relax
Here's a few of the less boring ones.

The Last Stand
5-26-06

A fool in a fools game
Lost in a death march through nice country
No way to describe
How extraordinary this experience is
Has been - and will be
In all the trillions of Planets and Stars
This may be the only place
That a semi conscious being
Can watch a Silver Hamburg rooster
Maul a hen twice his size
In their dance of renewal
What an incredible and
Unlikely experience I'm having
How infrequently I slowed down and notice
Today I will stay in gratitude
And cherish whatever time I have left

The Last Stand
5-28-06

Surrender all allusions of control
Change it if you can
Watch it if you can't
One show is just as good as another
They all reveal actions taken or omitted
Make a move
Pay the penalty
Reap the reward
Create gratitude the elixir the sustainer
The only sensible response
To the next thing
I will become a gratitude generator
For people-books-money
Spilled milk-
Computer music-
Broken truck
Homemade cheese and
Body temperature eggs
All is well

The Last Stand
7-8-06
Angry and depressed yesterday
How flawed and unreliable my
Mechanisms of perception and response
Take heart these kind of sensations
Only happened to living entities
And while there's life
There's hope for improvement
So today is the first and only time
I will experience July 8 1006
Make the best of it

The Last Stand
8-5-06

How little time I spend in awareness
Of what's going on in my head
Inpatients and hurry what's the rush
Are these Life long habits
Hardwired in my genetics
Or is it I haven't paid the price
In effort and concentration yet
Too much in a hurry to pay attention
To what ever I'm doing
Rush   rush   rush
There's nowhere to go
But I have to get there fast
Slowdown before you shut down
There is always only one project
As I write this I feel tension in my chest
Go take a shower

The Last Stand
8-29-06

Same freak show different day
Let humor coat
All my difficulties and inconveniences
I just experienced the best posture flow yet
It changes a little almost every workout
What a break coming to the planet earth
What a pain in the ass
Getting old and dead forever
So it goes
Grandfather said make a while the sunshine's
So now today I can make progress
Get just a little bit closer to
To a reliable self created harmonious head state
All these different theories
Mine is the same as Aristotle
All I know for sure is that I don't know
And I will never know
But I can continually know a little bit more
About the magnitude of my unknowing
Hello goodbye eat shit and die
But do it with a smile on your face
And gratitude in your heart

The Last Stand
11-2-06

Savor this instant
Stacking firewood-watching the dog run
A lot of crappy poker hands
Sunset and red wine
Savor the moments of my life
What incredible good fortune that
I blundered into this project of
Learning to create my own experience
The great work that I can practice
Anywhere
In fact the more screwed up things are
The more possibilities for progress
Not that I need any reason to get
Things screwed up
It seems to be
A natural skill I was born with
All is very well this morning

The Last Stand
11-3-06

So it's all over
All the way back to the primordial soup
Only in the opportunity of today
Do the consequences have any bearing
Like the track of a big snowball
Rolled up in a kids snowman project
Soon gone and forgotten
So many things to do
So little time
I came here in complete ignorance
And I'll leave in almost the same condition
But don't lose sight of
The only thing worth doing
Getting and keeping your head out of your ass
Press on there's not much time left

The Last Stand
11-19-06

I spent four hours playing
Internet poker last night
When did I ever spent four hours
Writing and drawing
Is all this writing and teaching bullshit
Just an old man's fantasy
Or will I pay the price and
Overcome laziness and momentum
Think how fulfilling it would be
To see someone
Make a positive change
Under my influence
If it's ever going to happen
Today is the day
Do it now

The Last Stand
1-10-07

THANK
What am I thinking about
Is this interpretation and reaction
Serve my only purpose
If I keep interpreting situations this way
And allowing the same reactions
Will I wind up where I think I want to be
Is this project even possible for me
Sounds like the Buddha pulled it off
And maybe Krishnamurti and Gurdjeiff
Really what's the likelihood
Zero if you don't keep trying
And zero + a little if I try as hard as I can
This shit isn't for the frightened or timid
Act boldly pay attention to each instance
If any form of disharmony starts to creep in
Tear it out in a loving peaceful way
And if you can't be loving and peaceful
Tear it the fuck out anyway
And then be loving and peaceful
I have climbed higher enough where I
Can see a small glow on the horizon
More later maybe

The Last Stand
3-31-07

The possibilities are larger
Than ever before
I can't do everything
But I can do something
With wisdom-integrity and power
What!!
All this chatter
About preparation is wearing Very thin
Pretty soon
I will be starting my eighth decade
I will get thin and stay fit
Control my thoughts
And for fill my destiny
And stop making excuses
If I intend to be a writer and teacher
Now is the time and this is the place

Commentary from August 30, 2014
To show you how ridiculous I am
I wrote something very similar
About a month ago
Only now it's my ninth decade
Creeping up on me
There is a strange kind of tenacity
In ignorance
But it's worked out for me
More than once before

The Last Stand
3-25-07

I read an article about Singapore this morning
A financially sound City state of 4 1/2 million
With reserves of 140 billion
And a balanced budget of 20 billion
I thought about my
Late night arrival at the Oriental Hotel
Without reservations
I was greeted by a well-spoken young woman
Who lead me to a very nice room on
The fifth floor
She beckon for me to sit on the couch
And offered to get me a drink
Then she opened a small portfolio and took my
Name address and credit card information
I've checked into hundreds of hotels
That was by far the classiest
VIP treatment for a disheveled
Middle aged vagabond with a backpack
A flood of memories of arose
A Tibetan refugee camp in Kathmandu
Where they chanted and made hand tied rugs
How airplanes land in the middle of Hong Kong
The cable car ride to Victoria Peak
And the hydrofoil to Macau
Traffic jams in Bombay and Bangkok
The Narrow gauge Mountain Railway
From Chiayi up to Alison in Taiwan

Fast action poker with a bunch
Of Greeks in Darwin Australia
The high-speed train
From Tokyo to Osaka
Or the slow coal burning steam engine
That went up to Yamagata
Watching a stream of man carrying
Bags of coal onto a small merchant ship
At the port in Manila
A scissor factory in a tent
Heated by wood scraps
Burnt in steel drums
On a cold January day South of Seoul
A high-altitude raft trip
Down the Eira Bamba
And an overnight stay at Machu Picchu
I haven't thought much about
Traveling in years

But this morning there's a new plan
Flying around my head
Get someone to stay here and
Take care of the animals
And buy two one-way tickets to
Johannesburg
Then make our way over land to Istanbul
Next day
In less than 24 hours the status quo
Laid waste to all of that

The Last Stand
4-10-07

Thinking about talking
So much goes in to the way it comes out
Energy level-emotional state
Status and style of the other person
Is there a lot to lose or gain
Lately I have been listening to myself more
And I spend a lot of time promoting my case
All the shit I got where I've been, who I know
I am as hungry now for recognition as I was
40 years ago when I was nowhere doing nothing
Is all this shit genetic or
Is there some chance I might grow up

The Last Stand
4-11-07

Thinking about self talking
Be silent and listen to the
Running commentary in my head
I'm hungry-this hurts-I got so much to do
I'll take care of that later
Why are they calling now
I have to call Fred
On and on and on all day long
I can't fix it but I can direct it
By paying attention to what I'm doing by
Bringing my thoughts back to where
I'm going
Or where I think I'm going or
Where I want to go

The Last Stand
4-14-07

Kurt Vonnegut died yesterday
And so it goes
Almost anything can happen
Usually the expected
But every once in a while
Is this going to be the day
The start of a brand-new way
Will I stop being unsettled
In a first rate settlement

The Last Stand
8-31-14

If you got this far it means either
You have a very boring life
Or you found some insights
Berried in all the gibberish
If you're not interested in
A bunch of theories about
Life extension and Optimal vitality
Skip the next few pages

DO NO HARM

Ingestion　　　inhalation　　　absorption
There are over 70,000 different chemicals
Commercially produced in the
United States today
Some very dangerous DDT-lead-mercury
Others quite helpful and some lifesavers
Very few have had any
Comprehensive safety analysis
They are used everywhere
In our food-clothes-building materials-furniture
Automobiles-skin creams-
Air fresheners-toothpaste
Hairspray-suntan lotions-bug spray
My theory is to try to avoid as many as possible
Even the ones that had extensive testing
That's most of the "medicines"
You see advertised on T V
I wrote a bunch of stuff about all the
different things to avoid
But I'm not going to include it here
Too boring
Here is the principle as I see it
Eliminate or strictly limit the chemical content
Of everything that you eat-breath or absorb

Food

Homegrown
On nutritionally rich organic soil
Nuts-seeds-vegetables-fruits and berries
Grass fed goat milk-cheese-yogurt
And butter
Organically fed free range
Chickens-eggs and beef
Organic coconut-olive and flaxseed oil's
Organically produced
Wine-beer and spirits

Second choice

Find local suppliers
With the same standards

Third choice

Same as above with
USDA organic certification

Land Mines

I tried but I just can't help listing a few of the
Worst things people are doing to themselves
Hydrogenated oil-rancid oil-corn oil-canola oil
Sugar-white flower-artificial-sweeteners

Commercially produced dairy and meat
This is truly a horror show
Quite often the new baby chicks are welcome
To the world by having their beaks torn off
Then fed inappropriate
And sometimes disgusting food
Jacked up on growth hormones and antibiotics
Crowded together in airplane hangar size barns
Never to breathe fresh air or see the light of day
In less than two months these poor creatures
Are sent off to the processing factory
I think about them when I look at our
Beautiful healthy chickens as they
Turn our gardens for us in the spring
By scratching for bugs and worms
Or how they like to take dust baths
In the ashes from our wood stove
You don't know what eggs are
Until you have had one
That went from the nesting box to
The frying pan

A Few Words About Cattle

Commercial beef production is just
As unwholesome as the poultry factories
Quite often
They are standing around feedlots
Ankle deep in feces urine and mud
Dining on totally
Inappropriate substances
Enhanced with antibiotics
And growth hormones
And slaughtered in less than half the time
Of there free range grass fed relatives
Think of all those the distress hormones
Surging through the future steaks

I think that supporting this
Is cruel and inhumane
Treatment of other living creatures is
Morally reprehensible and
Absolutely unnecessary
Eat locally grown
Humanely handled critters
If the Indians are correct about how we
Absorb the creatures spirit
As well their flesh Then
The hellish world
That is their only experience Of life
Is expressing itself and all the
Misery and depression
That people try to chase away with pills
It makes as much sense as a lot of my
Other half baked theories on things

Study
How to take care of myself
Financially   Mentally   Physically

Financially
Obtain the skills and knowledge
That enabled me to
Live in whatever lifestyle I choose
Without spending a lot of time
Making or managing money
Except when I run out
Or I get some kind of a crazy ass plan
And jumping I over my head
I think it's a genetic problem
But it has eased up quite a lot lately

Mentally
Learn and practice all the skills that go into
Creating a powerful harmonious experience
No matter what lady fortune is serving up
In that instant

Physically
Fitness-care and feeding
To obtain a level of optimum vitality
Is as long term and complicated
As learning how to keep
My head out of my ass (mental)

Strength
Isometrics-push ups-sit ups-thrusts-squats
Weightlifting? Not my choice

Endurance
Short periods of very intense activity
Biking-swimming-rowing-running
If you're young

Flexibility
Stretching any and all ways all day long

Yoga
I have been practicing steadily since 1979
Take some classes and practice

Here's my theory on optimal vitality
All it takes is: maintain
A harmonious mind state

Get enough sleep
Stay hydrated with chemical-free water
Eat wholesome organic food

Stay trim and fit
Continually
Study and try to figure things out
Until it's over

The last bull shit from the last stand

9-15-14
I was laying in bed this morning thinking
How quickly I can get angry at our cat
When he's hungry or wants to go out
He howls at me in a very loud voice
And I get this strong urge to crush
His head in the door when he's leaving
It's been about 40 years since
I first read meditations by Markus Aurelius
And I have pretty consistently written and
Thought about fixing my head since then

I spent hundreds of hours talking
To four different shrinks
Weekend and week-long workshops
Whenever I drive along or '
Work around the house
I listen to tapes or recently podcasts
Ram Dass-Joseph Campbell-
Tony Robbins-Napoleon Hill-
Robert DeRopp-Joseph Goldstein
Piles and piles of books-hardly any fiction
Tom Clancy and Kurt Vonnegut
= 95% of my fiction reading
Group therapy sessions-
Yoga weekend intensives

I am drawing up on the end of
My 75th year
And my best shot was
Wanting to kill the house cat
So I decided to get up but
I couldn't find my glasses
I didn't want to turn on the light and
Disturb my wife
It took me about 5 minutes of peaceful
Feeling around to find them
Then I remembered the spilled wine
On the porch last week
And the peaceful good humor
I experienced
As I picked up the
Broken glass and cleaned up the wine
Even 5 years ago
This would not have been possible for me
I have made a lot of progress
But there's still quite a way to go
I am as determined as ever that
I'll fix my head before I am dead
I hope you found something of value
In all this noise and confusion

Most Important Books in My Life

Meditations by Marcus Aurelius
Think and Grow Rich by Napoleon Hill
The Master Game by Robert De Ropp
Insight Meditation by Joseph Goldstein
Self Mastery by Swami Paramananda
Unlimited Power by Anthony Robbins
Success System that Never Fail by WC Stone
Miracles Wisdom books Inc.
View from the Real World by G. I. Gurdjieff
In Search of the Miraculous by P.D. Ouspensky
40 years After Gurdjieff John Fuchs
The Flight of the Eagle Krishnamurti
Erroneous Zones by Wayne Dyer
Crush It by Gary Vaynerckuk
4-Hour Work Week by Tim Ferriss
Atlas Shrugged by Ayn Rand
Tales of Power by Carlos Castaneda
Power Versus Force by David Hawkins
Siddhartha by Hermann Hess
The Power of Thought
by Omraam Mikhael Aivanhov

Resources

http://www.NaturalNews.com
http://www.AlsearsMD.com
http://www.Trans4Mind.com
http://www.FourHourWorkWeek.com
http://www.BulletProofExec.com
http://www.TrippLanier.com

The last three have really great Podcasts
available from their website or at iTunes

For a quick and simple
Exercise routine try
LifeEvents.org

Take a look at by blog
http://BoneYardExpress.blogspot.com

Information

2014

Published by
Boneyard Express
4 Market St
Oneonta N Y
13820
TheBoneYardExpress.com

607 434 3429

Thanks to Swami Sadashiva Tirtha
http://TheHipGuru.com

and Louise Jerensen

ISBN-13: 978-0692312520

Greenearthoneonta.com
4 Market St Oneonta NY
13820

Notes

Made in the USA
Middletown, DE
07 August 2015